from SHADING SIGNS PETS IN SPIRIT

An Adult Coloring Book to Help
Identify Signs from Pets in Heaven

by Authors
Lyn Ragan and Dorothy Pigue

Cover and Book Design by *Lyn M Oney*
Illustrations © Lyn Ragan and Dorothy Pigue

Trade paper ISBN 978-1-946223-90-6

To all of our beloved Pets in Heaven,
With Unconditional Love
and Beautiful Grace…

Introduction

Lyn Ragan lost the *love of her life* in 2008. One second they were chatting on the phone and in the next, he was killed while preparing for work.

Her grief spiraled into a web of sadness she found difficult to break free of. All of their future dreams destroyed and her life altered forever, Lyn was taken by surprise when she started receiving communications from her deceased fiancé— via dreams. Ms. Ragan would later write about their visits and eventually publish several books on the subject of *Afterlife Communications*.

Her mission in life is to help those who grieve from the loss of a loved one; her ultimate goal to replace painful grief with belief and understanding. Lyn works tirelessly helping those she can reach to understand this physical life is not the end of who we are, and that love and life lives forever— as do our Souls.

Dorothy Pigue was born into a family of clairvoyants. As a young child, she began hearing the voices of spirits around her. It took many years for Dorothy to realize she could communicate with the spirit world and with loved ones who have crossed over. Wanting to enhance her gifts and psychic abilities, she trained with Carl Woodall at the *Atlanta Metaphysical Center* in Atlanta, Georgia, and became a graduate of *The Anastasi System of Psychic Development* in 2014.

Dorothy is also a Master Herbalist who has been practicing as a Korean Medicine Woman since 1996. She is a Clinical Certified Hypnotherapist, a Certified Usui/Holy Fire Reiki ® Practitioner, and an author.

Dorothy's mission in life is to share her gifts and abilities in hopes of removing the *pain of grief*. Healing begins with love and from the other side, *Love* is the message she enjoys sharing.

Authors Lyn Ragan and Dorothy Pigue are excited to come together on a personal undertaking to help bring peace, love, and healing into the hearts of those who grieve.

Our Wish For You…

*S*igns and symbols from beloved pets are seen by thousands every day. From the other side, our beloved fur-children use signs to connect with family they left behind on this earthly plane. Oftentimes, the gifts they share are unseen or are difficult to identify.

Learning to speak the Language of Spirit requires practice but once a message is identified, the joy of hearing from your Pet in Heaven can bring great comfort. This coloring book can help you in identifying your signs, your messages, and your symbols from your beloved Pet.

Our wish is to help you cope with your loss, witness your special sign, and receive *healing* at the same time. That is why we produced this coloring book. Each illustration on the following pages is associated with thousands of documented communications from around the world.

From our personal experiences, we believe each one of these signs is a dynamic blueprint of acceptance, healing, and witnessing messages from our beloved pets. Signs from our fur-kids are normally very gentle. By their given nature, they do not demand a response nor do they direct us to take an action. Through their appearance however, we are given a spiritual reveal or what we like to describe as— *A BIG HUG FROM HEAVEN*.

Our hope is that these coloring pages will not only help to heal your broken spirit, but also help you in identifying the continued love you receive from your fur-child in Heaven. Remember— there are no rulebooks or time limits for your grief. Take all the time you need.

One step, one day, and one coloring page… at a time.

Love lives forever, and so do our SOULS.

The Butterfly

Butterflies are messengers of the moment.
These wonders of nature are remarkable symbols.
The Butterfly embodies the process
of transformation and is a very
popular sign by our fur-children
in the Afterlife.
When our pets choose
the Butterfly as their sign of choice,
their message is a very beautiful one…
"Yes, I'm right here.
Please talk to me.
Tell me how you're feeling.
I can hear you.
I'm right here to help
ease your sorrow."
Across the veil into
the Afterlife,
***Love** is everything.*

The Butterfly

The Dragonfly

A very powerful messenger,
the Dragonfly is full of mysticism,
magic, and powers of illusion.
They remind us to bring more lightness
and joy into our world.
They carry the wisdom of change
and adaptability in life.
When our pets choose
the Dragonfly
as their sign of choice,
their message is a loving one…
"Yes, I'm here with you.
Talk to me.
Share everything with me
for I haven't gone anywhere.
I can hear you."

The Dragonfly

The Black Crow

When the Black Crow brings
a message from a beloved pet,
it is a profound confirmation
and symbol of "rebirth".
Our pets use the crow to tell us
they are dwelling in the past,
the present, and the future
all at the same time.
Their message is beautiful
and crystal clear...
"I am crow, master of illusion
and keeper of sacred law.
Come share with me
the magic that I explore...
our continued soul connection."

The Black Crow

Feathers

When angels are near,
feathers appear.
It's really quite true.
It takes a special moment,
a sacred space,
to see the beauty of a divine feather.
Our pets in spirit place feathers
in our path
at just the right time
to offer love, validation, and comfort.
When your beloved fur-babe chooses
the feather as their sign,
their message is a comforting one…
"Yes, I'm here. Right here, with you.
Right where I always
want to be."

Feathers

Coins from Heaven

Whether it's a penny,
a nickel, a dime, or a quarter,
the coin you find can be a GIFT
from your fur-child.
No matter where you locate
your sign,
the message from your sweet pet
is quite clear...
"I am always with you.
You never have to worry,
because you are
never alone."

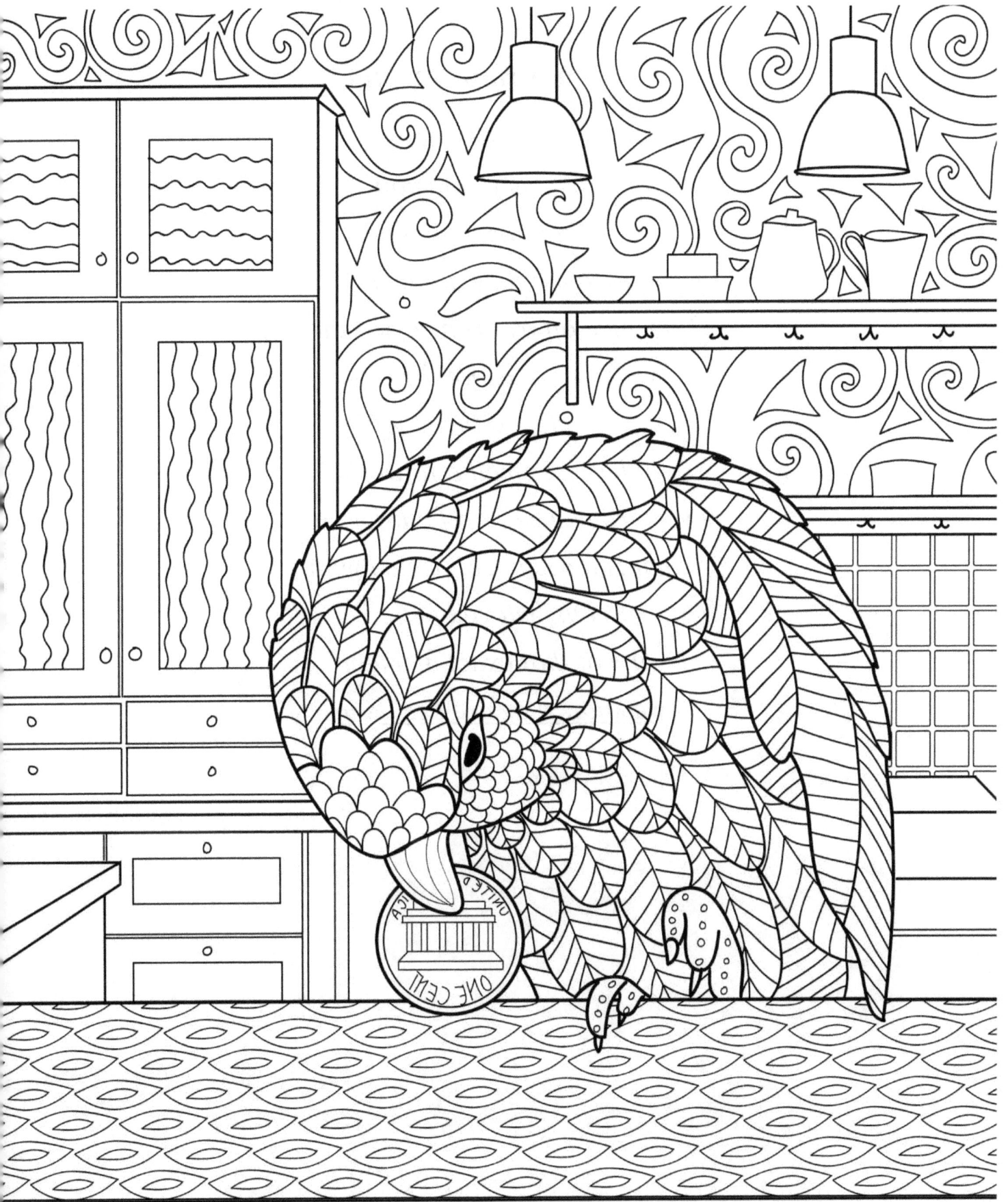

Coins From Heaven

Scents From Beyond

Scents and smells
are a very common
way that our loving pets
let us know they are around.
They give off fragrances we know
we can't question because
we've smelled them before.
When we smell a flower's
sweet fragrance or a familiar scent
that is directly connected with
our beloved pet,
it's at that exact moment
<u>we know they are beside us</u>.

Scents fron Heaven

Angel Numbers

Becoming aware and watching
for number signs
helps direct a path
where spirit
(your beloved fur-child)
becomes your guide.
Numbers are an easy way
for our pets
to grab our attention.
When your fur-child delivers
an angel number to you,
their message is very clear…
"If you only knew how much
you are loved and adored.
I am so proud to be here—
<u>with you.</u>"

Angel Numbers

999

888

555

333

222

777

444

666

111

The Hummingbird

When our loyal companions send us
this incredible sign,
(the hummingbird)
they are in essence transporting
their unconditional love,
devotion, and phenomenal beauty
directly from the Heavens above.
When your fur-child chooses
the Hummingbird
as their sign for you,
the message they share
is incredibly special…
"Our love conquers anything;
even death.
I'm here, with you."

The Hummingbird

The Ladybug

The ladybug symbolizes
love and protection
and is a very popular sign
by our devoted companions
in the Afterlife.
These little wonders of nature
are remarkable Gifts
from our beloved pets
in Heaven.
Because on the other side,
Love *is everything...*

The Ladybug

Dream Visitations

Dreaming about our pets
is a very common experience.
Because we're sleeping,
we are in that in between place
that links our earthly bodies
to the spirit world.
Dream Visitations overflow
with peace and love.
Our very special pets,
here and on the other side,
only want for one thing...
to let us know their love
<u>*is unconditional*</u>*.*

Dream Visitations

Cloud Formations

When we open our hearts and minds,
we become aware of the energetic
pull that attracts our attention.
Cloud formations are tailored
specifically for each person
and for their needs at that very moment.
When your beloved pet shapes
a Cloud Formation as their gift to you,
they share a magnificent message...
"The love we have cannot
be measured.
Please believe in me
and trust that I am with you...
always."

Cloud Formations

Moving Objects

Sometimes our sweet pets
move objects to get our attention.
Things that mean something to us,
or to them,
can be repositioned strategically
to make us seek and find
the article in question.
When your pet wants your attention,
they will go to great lengths
to master their communication.
Even if they have
to repeat it several times—
before you get it.

Red Cardinal

In this circle of life,
the Red Cardinal reminds you
of the importance of
yourself as an individual.
You are loved
and divinely adored.
When your fur-child delivers
a Red Cardinal
as their preferred gift,
they share a very beautiful message…
"I'm right here with you.
When you think of me,
please know I am beside you,
giving you warmth and strength.
I love you."

The Whale

An ancient symbol for creation—
be it of the body or the world—
the Whale reminds us to honor
our soul's purpose.
They tell us to claim the Destiny
that we know is already ours.
When your fur-child shares the Whale
as their sign of choice,
their message is quite powerful...
"Embrace the unknown.
I am here, even if you can't see me.
Trust my signs to guide you."

The Whale

The Dolphin

The Dolphin reminds us to
listen to our unique voice,
our amazing intuition.
Their appearance tells us
to be open to new experiences.
When your beloved pet chooses
the Dolphin as their sign for you,
their message is a BIG one...
"Enjoy this moment, for it shall not
pass this way again.
It's time to breathe new life into yourself.
Get out. Play. And explore.
I'll be right there with you."

The Dolphin

Horse Messenger

The Horse is closely tied to
"New Beginnings" as Souls
ride into and out of the worlds, upon it.
Teaching you how to ride into new directions
to "awaken" your personal freedom
and power, the Horse brings with it...
new journeys.
When your beloved fur-child chooses
the Horse as their sign of choice,
they share a wonderful message...
"You are free to take your power back.
Your new Journey is now.
Don't worry, I'll be with you—
every step of the way."

Horse Messenger

The Squirrel

Masters at preparing,
the Squirrel reminds us always
to make time to socialize
and play.
When our beloved pets choose
the Squirrel as their sign for us,
their message is a great one...
"Have more fun and don't take
this life so seriously.
Find the beauty in Life again.
I'm here helping you."

The Squirrel

The Deer

The Deer brings you new opportunities
and opens doors to great adventures.
They remind you to be gentle with yourself
and to continue to seek for
your inner treasures.
When our beloved pet chooses the Deer
as their gift of choice,
they share a wonderful message...
"I am with you, giving you my guidance.
Follow my signs...
I will always show you the way."

The Deer

The Hawk

The Hawk's broad vision
allows them to see what the future holds.
They signify joining together
with all that is.
Bringing communications from the spirit world,
the Hawk is a superior messenger.
When your beloved fur-child chooses the Hawk
as their sign of choice,
your message is quite beautiful...
"Please know that your enlightenment
is imminent. I am here. And I love you.
Take me with you."

The Hawk

The Pet Rat

The Rat informs us
to take up a new hobby.
By learning something new,
we learn to challenge ourselves.
They remind us to be the best that we can be.
When your beloved pet chooses the Rat
as their sign of choice,
their message is a clear one…
"Let go of yesterday.
It's okay to move closer to your dreams.
Today is a new beginning."

The Pet Rat

The Fish

When the Fish enters
your life, it will often signal
one of the senses being awakened:
visions, prophetic dreams, or clairaudience.
The Fish teaches us to adapt
and streamline our lives.
When your beloved pet chooses the Fish
as their sign for you,
their message is a wonderful one...
"Together, we continue our creative elements in this life.
And together, we awaken your dreams.
I will always be with you.
Always."

The Fish

The Dog

The energy of the Dog is always reminding us
to be loyal and truthful to ourselves.
It is important to love who we are
in order to be of assistance to others.
When you fur-baby chooses the Dog
as their sign of choice,
their message is a beautiful one...
"You are not alone.
Allow me to help you and to guide you.
I will always be with you.
There's no other place I'd rather be."

The Dog

The Cat

The Cat reminds you to trust your intuition.
They tell you it's time to
believe in yourself.
You have everything you need in your life,
right now,
to make your dreams come true.
When your beloved pet shares the Cat
as their sign of choice,
their message is quite clear…
"Trust yourself.
You see my signs.
My clues are with you everywhere you go.
I'm here—with you."

The Cat

The Rabbit

*The Rabbit shows you how
to notice the signs around you.
They can help you recognize
the tides of movement in your life,
and can enable you
to become even more creative
in your world.
When your sweet pet in Heaven shares the Rabbit
as their sign of choice,
their message is a great one...
"Your energy is spot on right now.
Know that I am here and am helping you.
What we start today,
will be greatly rewarded tomorrow."*

Rabbit

The Chipmunk

Synchronicity is in the air
when we see the Chipmunk.
Teaching us that Spirit
(your beloved pet)
is always close,
the Chipmunk encourages us
to ask for help and guidance.
Now is a perfect time to ask for a sign.
Believe in magic.
When your beloved fur-child shares the Chipmunk
as their sign for you,
their message is a special one...
"Something good is on it's way.
Something that will light up your heart.
I can't wait to see you smile...
again."

Chipmunk

Hearts

When signs or symbols come into our lives
from our beloved fur-kids,
they each carry a beautiful message.
It's a very personal and usually profound
announcement and one where
the Heart symbol is an amazing
communication of love.
When your beloved pet chooses the Heart
as their sign for you,
their message is extraordinary...
"Love is the key ingredient to life and to us.
From my heart to yours,
know and trust the magnitude of our connection.
I am here. I adore you.
I love you."

Hearts

Flowers

Flowers speak a beautiful and timeless language.

They carry spiritual meanings and can convey many

messages from the beyond.

A gift of a flower(s) can melt your heart

and even open your mind

to something unseen.

When your beloved pet chooses

a Flower as their sign for you,

their message is a heartfelt one...

"I just adore you.

Please accept this flower as my way of saying,

'Our love continues on forever.

Together we will be,

again one day."

Flowers

The Eagle

Eagles are symbols
of great power, timing, and freedom.
To accept the energy of this magnificent bird
is to accept the new and powerful dimension
coming in your life with a new
and heightened responsibility
to your spiritual growth.
It's time to discover
your personal power.
When your beloved fur-babe shares
the Eagle as their sign of choice,
their message is a Grand One...
"Like a beacon, your heart knows the way.
It's time to shine your light, my loved one.
Don't worry—I'm here to help you."

The Eagle